MOCKINGBIRD

Mockingbird

DEREK WEBSTER

THE POETRY IMPRINT AT VÉHICULE PRESS

Published with the generous assistance of The Canada Council for the
Arts and the Canada Book Fund of the Department of Canadian Heritage,
and the Société de développement des entreprises culturelles du Québec
(SODEC)

Funded by the Government of Canada
Financé par le gouvernement du Canada | Canadä

SIGNAL EDITIONS EDITOR: CARMINE STARNINO

Cover design: David Drummond
Set in Filosofia and Minion by Simon Garamond
Printed by Marquis Book Printing Inc.

Dépôt légal, Library and Archives Canada and the
Bibliothèque national du Québec, third trimester 2015.

LIBRARY AND ARCHIVES CANADA CATALOGUING IN PUBLICATION

Webster, Derek, 1970-, author
Mockingbird / Derek Webster.

Poems.
Issued in print and electronic formats.
ISBN 978-1-55065-426-4 (paperback). – ISBN 978-1-55065-433-2 (epub)

I. Title.

PS8645.E254M62 2015   C811'.6   C2015-903063-3
C2015-903064-1

Published by Véhicule Press, Montréal, Québec, Canada
www.vehiculepress.com

Distribution in Canada by LitDistCo
www.litdistco.ca

Distributed in the U.S. by Independent Publishers Group
www.ipgbook.com

Printed in Canada on FSC certified paper.

For my family

CONTENTS

The Orphan

It's a cold comfort, sleeping in.
Without friends. And beds
are deep places to sink into.
You cannot bury yourself there
no matter how you try.
Your small life wants to live in you
despite everyone's attempts to do it in.
The day holds out no hand to you
now your mother's gone.

I like to lull myself to sleep
and turn to her. No one else
will guard her as she sleeps. So I
must stay here, lonely, by her side,
if not in body then at least in mind,
my task simple, clear as rain:
to hear my mother's voice, high and thin.
And then the morning can begin.

1

Calendar

February, defenses lowered,
our chats commodious, neither bored.

Then March Break, two wooden boats,
barreled limes, chorus of goats.

April, a pleated girlish professor
lectures in the bushes, against a pillar.

May says two working stiffs can have.
Your flowering bean, "Zbigniew."

Then summer's thunderous dressing gown
floods the field and heart with wine.

September's grey daughter culls the land,
urgency in your scribbled hand.

October: three baby gourds.
Mute goblins, faceless hoards.

You scrub every surface with Fantastik.
November's newspapers still in their plastic.

December, stray dog crouched in the yard.
Sarcastic mail addressed to "The Bard."

Walking into a cold, blue wind.
Calendar says, It's January, friend.

After the Break-Up

I was beside myself, living alone
in the country where my grandfather lived
in a farmhouse built with five or six in mind.

I didn't have a job, and felt the shame
of one too young to understand the gift
of time. I wanted to be seen and loved

for who I thought I was, or might be soon.
I went for walks, read about war. How hollow
my days seemed. Boring: I was boring.

The Highland cattle, chewing and staring
in the leased fields next door, became my proof
that I was there, and still worth looking at.

Anger scared me, especially my own,
so I threw orange tennis balls against
a cinderblock divide behind the house

whenever the silence became too much.
In the fall dark, I saw the form that fed
the cows. It never talked to me, just turned

to look—did not resume his work—until
I'd trudged far past the field. Young men are seen
as dangerous, no matter who they want

to be, or the beauty of their partial thoughts.
It took a dream for me to leave that place:
profiles against the sky, a lantern's eye,

robins plunging beaks into my body's
field, tugging worms. And me evicted Caliban,
a borrower, not owner of the land.

Floating World

We spend the evening gliding down the Seine
under brass angels and the partially insane

who look down on us without a word.
Food arrives: lamb cuts on an oak board.

The camembert has soured. (I swallow "because.")
She does her best Napoleon

for the psycho-motor therapist down the bench.
Shortly I will offer up my passable Wellington.

O when did we start disbelieving?
Outside, dawn windows, each lit by a candle.

I can almost see her face, pearl-grey,
her bare white feet, her knees lightly skinned.

Err

A baby's squall
Brawling seagull

Child whining
Door creaking

Dog locked out
Electric saw's first bite

Cat licking plastic bib
Don Juan with a wooden leg

Daytime squeeze
Mounting sneeze

Rat moving at your feet
A car in the street

Fertilizer newly spread
Wafts from the acrid bed

Wife I thought I knew
Starting again with you

Self-Timed Photograph

The window's too bright
in the dark wall of the unfurnished room

with its distant golden dome,
the bright, false starts littering the table.

My arms crossed. No smile in my
girl-zapped head. I was wound so tight,

I hardly know me anymore,
I'm a stranger, someone I've never met,

but still an occupant of that rented room,
watering the dirt, waiting for the bloom.

Moving Day

She liked it here: perched on a cul-de-sac,
wind on her eyelids.

A softer jaw. Glow of a dead star.
Learn to love what is hidden.

Below, the canopies unfurl. The sky darkens.
Rain-dust, the colour of her eyes.

Larkinesque

Online dating's huge-breasted ad
fills my screen next to "Home is so Sad."

He'd smirk at the clash, Hull's divine moper,
remember again some hothouse encounter:

"Across the ponds, toads and gentlemen
mount their scummed lovers' reflection."

Or: "Amidst lime weeds, no one sees
the busty wallflower's scaly knees."

Then the suppressed, too-Yeatsian lines:
"Write me songs of salt and iron,

life sans love drowns in longing—"
                                        Ugh.
No more poetic moonlighting.

Nine months single, I still smell
you. On the bed. Your lost green shirt.

Warm and viral, home dies
quietly, into dusk and hurt.

Intervention

Snowy winter morning. Quiet house
on a quiet street. Two cars pull up: one bears
the local coat of arms. A plain-looking man
gets out of the other, mounts the steps, looks around.
Keys jingle. He unlocks the door, enters
the hall, adjusts a picture that's gone askew.
A woman appears. A child sits on the stairs.

"You can't come in," she says.

                    He looks around.

          "Can't a man visit his own home?" he says.

"Not you. Not after what you've done to me.
You're supposed to call ahead. Why are you here,
what do you want?"

               "You know why. The judge said."

"I won't leave," she says, trembling. "I don't know how."
She grabs the boy. "Not here. Not now."

                              "Let go.
          There are rules for days like this. No more delays.
          And don't even think about getting physical.
          Two cops are waiting outside, in case you have
          another violent change of heart."

"No, no. My little man, he matters more—
I need to keep him. Who will walk him to school?"

"All the times you were out of your head,
I fed him, read him stories, brushed his teeth—"

"You never did those things when I was well.
I saw. I was there. I know what I know."

> "Do you know you need to clean your veins? Do you
> know our world runs better when you're gone?
> I can't say where you go—and I don't care.
> We don't need you to put your dime bag in.
> It's already been decided, you can't stop it.
> What's best for him is my concern—"

> "For now!
Why are you so cruel to me? So hateful,
so unmoved?"

> "Amy, I know you too well.
> Your problems bury us like winter drifts.
> Every night, another foot of pure white hurt
> falls in the dark, smothering us. Your problems
> bury everything else, even the things
> that I've done wrong."

> "It's you! It's always you!
Why did you leave me? I need to know."

> "I've told you—"

"Tell me again."

> "What, tell you what you've done?
> Should we go through your purse, your closet drawers?
> Why must I prove your own actions to you?
> You lie. You drink. Deny. Say it's all my fault.
> And now the pills. You won't change. You need help."

"To hear you say it now, it sounds so simple.
But you drank too, back then—much more than me.
God keep me from men like you. You've treated me
like a broken toy, an embarrassment
ever since I shared my past with you.
Truth is, you're not strong enough for marriage.
If I'm so bad, why did you marry me?"

> "I wanted you—it's painful to admit—
> because of your effect on other men.
> Your beauty made them envy me,
> made me feel powerful, a somebody.
> People looked at me a second time
> with you on my arm. I liked that look, could see
> the perfect couple mirrored in their eyes."

"HA! You're the one in need of help, not me.
A woman should be treated with respect,
not thrown out like trash when she's lost her use."

> "We could have made things work if—
> enough. That's over, someone else's life.
> I won't argue. There's no *we* left in us."

She drops to her knees, begins to sob. The child
leaves his hiding place on the stairs, runs down
to hug and soothe his mother, a new role
he'll play for years to come, her protector
from anything that makes her hurt herself.

"You still don't know who you are. Nothing has changed.
Why tell me now? What are you hiding from me?"

> "A small thing happened. Early one morning
> in the winter kitchen. I was half-asleep

when I reached for the pantry door and it half-
fell off, the top hinge ripped out of the wall.
And I remembered why—the fight we'd had
the week before, when you threw that glass weight
at my head, and I punched the dented door
in anger. That morning, I saw us. Saw
the bare, brown shelves. The bruises. That's what we were.
The truth returned like a prodigal son
I never knew I had, welcomed with tears.
I had to hug him tightly. I had to leave."

"Every sound and shape your mouth makes—lies.
You said you were by my side. But all along
you'd left, abandoned me on a far shore."

                    "I'm being more honest than you ever have."

"You only think you are. I hate your lying."

                    "Why do you lash out, again and again?
                    I begged and pleaded with you to talk, to find
                    out what was wrong—"

Remembering his purpose here, he halts.

                                        "Enough. It's time."

The boy moves closer to his mother, sensing
a change in the air, bad things to come.

                    "Let go," his father says, pulling his little
                    arms from around his sagging mother's neck.
                    Holding on, the boy resists. "Robby, I—"

From the ground, she looks up, wailing, beseeching:

"Oh, let's leave town together and not come back!
I might have brought this on myself. But I can't
help it. Everything hurts when love breaks down."

Boy and father struggle. The bigger wins.

"Do you love me still?" she asks. "Tell me why not.
If I changed, became stronger, learned to control—"

        "We've stumbled toward this moment for years.
        Please don't make me call the police inside."

She doesn't answer. Silence makes them pause.
She sighs and trembles. A formal feeling comes.
The boy watches the change in his mother's face.

        "What are you thinking of?" the man asks his wife.

She wipes her nose, speaks quietly.
"About the country. Nights when I'd stay up
smoking on the balcony, and the moon
would rise over the lake. I loved to hear
the nervous creatures murmur in the dark."

        He knows it's time. She won't try to stop him now.
        "Give mommy a hug." He leads his son away.

"I'll write to you, okay?" The boy nods, not
knowing what that means. They walk through the door.

        The father turns, wants to say "I'll visit you"—

but finds he cannot speak. For still kneeling
on the floor, his wife is being swallowed alive
by swirling, inky clouds of smoke. Quickly,

the triangle of her body disappears.
Only her face and eyes remain, staring
at faithless him, outward from their prisons.

Where Are You Now?

Where are you now?
I heard you left town.

I thought of you, as a man dug up
Byzantine galleons on TV.

I saw your clothes for sale
in a thrift-store window.

Someone said you had kids
or was that a dream—

someone read me your obituary
or was *that* a dream—

was that you, running across the mountain,
small red hood, quick feet?

I hope so. That would suggest
you're still among the living

and not the deep, forgetful river
rising around me.

Necklace

The neck's lace
and heart's continent.

Churning, underwater clouds,
each stone suspended in its hour.

When we're no longer together,
strung with leather,

devotion will survive.
Apparent, alive.

2

Flushing the Groundhog

He's a mini-market manager with a big man's
coat and a habit of neglecting his bills.
Collectors have been hired to send
him up the Yangtze, tin-can his errant
nightly thievery. Acts vigilant. He's green,
all squint. Thinks his castle's secure
with three dull, hefted shovels
cocked not ten feet away. Nod. A rock
in the bush misdirects him—*Exit,*
pursued by a bear. His furious
galumph's a small perk of the job.

Strung up out back, his begging
symmetrical paws are instructive.
He looks like he split town in a froth
then had a thunderbolt—some business
he forgot, so important
it makes him close his eyes.
The death takes its time.

His arrogant coat ripped off, he's
like everybody: mortgage unpaid,
lawn growing longer, a rabbit
with stunted legs. No parting
note for the wife—just a red stain on the doorstep.
His plump, tawny offspring will cry
and forget him. Someone asks why
we had to do it right before winter.
I'm not the one to answer that question.

Woodcutter

Faded blue track suit with paint stains
to the big pile under the pines
carrying the good axe with the red head.

Boys go get the wheelbarrow.
Dump it sideways so the wood falls flat.
Stack it out the length of the garage.

If it rise too high, replenish the second row.
If the head gets stuck, lift the whole log
and crash it right down on the block.

It that don't split it, get the blue sledgehammer.
Turn the log over, tap in the wedge
and split the stubborn bugger end to end.

Canning Time

Baby cucumbers lifted from the garden.
Tomatoes, peppers cooked with onion.
Strawberries boiled in pectin.

The mother worked, the child watched.
For each thing, a jar from the box.
Pour the melted wax on top.

Across the counter, a regiment of jars
Conveyed, without a word, downstairs.
Stacked three deep. And still there.

What is a Watershed?

Like petals from the cherry tree,
we will always have more words.

High among mountains, along
a quiet line, fallen water without
choice runs to one side or another.

She-Wolf

Three-sided ears that
swivel like an office chair.
If you walked past, hours earlier,
she knows you were here,
smells the soap you washed
your throat with, and the stains
in your underwear. Glimpsed
through grey posts, one eye's playful
but shows a glint of fear—like a father-figure
tried bashing in her head with a brick
and failed—while the other, narrowed
like an arrow-slit in a high tower,
notes your bramble-scratched ear.

She moves briskly, her limbs
a history of travel. The fur
around her neck bristles
like shark-skin, down to the sexy,
muscular curve of her rump
that coils and jumps from worlds away
—or saunters off across the hills
for no reason you can understand.
She will look at you, run, appraise or hunt,
and does not care
that you think of her when she's not there.

Emily Dickinson

My life was mine—an uncut book—
Shelved until the day
A reader passed—and snagged—
And carried me away

And now we slink—the sidewalks—
And now rob—Peter Pan—
And every phrase he pilfers
Reminds me—who I am—

And when he sighs—at midnight
Over the—yawning—page
I brush his temple—kiss
His vaulting architrave

All my rival—volumes—
Dislike my—acid—tongue—
But I don't rest—to wag
Or fear their—alkaline—

The day he yawns—I'll slip
Onto a lower shelf—
Until I'm—pinched—in secret—
Become another's—wife—

Verlaine

Beneath a fake-mink trap
she said, "Yeah, do me like that"
and swore. What a foul-mouthed girl
he was. Knew how to make it pay
better than nouveau Beaujolais.
Knew when to curse me, call me sir.

Kicked out by his father,
no contact with his mother
since "the incident downtown"—
she murdered steaks chez granny,
dressed like a 30s tranny
and loved to lounge around.

She'd boil hot dogs
nights she worked the park bogs
then slide home on the black ice,
shouldering her issues
like a thousand one-blow tissues.
Now wouldn't that be nice.

She had a twisted sense of mercy,
the way a new star eats a star nursery
or the moon—thinner,
brighter, more fastidious—
will let its shadows chase us
howling quietly for dinner.

On hot summer nights
she'd meet Mr. Wight
who heavy petted, she said, so well
she drank the Kool-Aid

and dressed like a chambermaid
until she cried like kittens down a well.

A drunk old friend
said, "See you round the bend"
and chewed his tequila worm
but Verlaine never made it back.
John Solo unzipped her stomach
to keep a friend warm.

Lying in the dawn park,
her face frowned. A meadowlark
chose that moment to sing.
I know know know him.
How did it happen.
The EMTs said nothing.

Beneath his fake-mink trap
no one did her like that anymore.
Just a witty, mixed-up boy.
Verlaine could make it pay
better than nouveau Beaujolais.
Knew when to curse them, call them sir.

Ted Hughes

Crow jumps down from post and wire,
inspects a field shorn of grass and briar.
Its walk is a mix of chicken

and the smug strut of a roguish squire,
unrepentant, tarred and feathered,
as if it's just nailed some milkmaid.

It upends rocks with stab and flick.
Beetles flee between its feet.
But it feels watched: the straw man's armed.

Coal lids closed, it leaps into air.
Giant shadow rows. Outside the dream
someone knifes the dreamer.

The Black Lake

A wicked joke—

he waded in, then
all went black.

Dove deeply to words
and painted images,

the lakebed a shoe
with no foot kicking.

Like a call through glass
I heard my name repeated,

his hair floating,
the new world reaching,

all thought held
like unfallen rain,

green as the day.
Then, bright iron

sliding from the lake,
and each drop

a thrust, a bomb.
The legend underway.

Nursery Rhyme for Big Brother

Palace flags and shoot-to-kill orders,
cardboard tanks and well-lit borders,
dungeons and lice, grenades and books,
photos retouched and high-kicking boots,
bright deadly frogs, bureaucratic snails,
land-reform talks that never fail to fail,
gas in the mountains, *e-coli* in the food,
gold chocolate fountains and light sweet crude.

Do you dream of rending wrong from right?
Good luck, my darling, good luck and good night.

Bridge

One thought of walking
over a bridge together

twenty years ago
No talk

Sun- and un-lit waves
and light traffic

and the river flowing
One thinks of walking

with nothing to say
but "the sunlight

flowed over and away"
Today is a bridge

to one thought of walking

Great Black Wasp

Its tail-barb scraped
my cheek,

then it stung me,
startled the air,
and landed far off

on the window's blue sky,
a winged keyhole
moving down the glass—

Sphex pensylvanicus,
the purple darkness
that renders wordless—

then flew off to repeat itself
under earth or in wall,
attach itself
to my paralyzed hypotheses,

talk to itself endlessly
through the paper wall,
turn the things I miss
into what I am.

Night Game

Homeruns can save. The bases clear,
the windup monolithic as the year

you shook and cried, and it rained chords
of music dreamt by underlords.

And from the far field a grey voice is tossed
just like before, though struck anew by loss,

and a low shape calling you from a hill
says you can make it. You're coming home still.

3

Bird Catcher

I close my eyes among the trees
when the sun is high. Shadows and birds
return at twilight. And so do I,
to pull their delicate clawed feet
from my nets, and set them in cages
to sell at market on Saturdays.

But at night, in dreams, they fly away
at smart sharp angles, cutting aloft,
and I am trapped in my own craft.
What a dull brown bird I am.
I must learn to escape myself,
live in the tops of evergreens.

The Hunter

This modest valley of false shepherds
is full of grafted fruit:
strange throat, new fingers, old eyes,

plastic heart. I don't know
where I'm from, or who
sends the orders to kill.

I raise my bow, let harrowing fly,
take songs from dead hands,
tramp home to weed the anthologies

and slowly acquire the gist of song.
Other hunters find
my holes, build nests in my loins.

Hotel Pianist

When the ladies want pictures
they drape their arms around me.
Save me, they whisper.
And I do.

Rocks glasses tinkle on the bar.
The beautiful young man
dances with a white-wine pensioner.
He'll leave you, I sing.
And he does.

Widower

Red pears, the bucket tipped over.
It all gets thrown away.

It's winter now. Why are you standing in the street?
Your bones gleaming through your skin.

Spring. Amazing, a pitcher on the dresser:
pink light, grey ice, blue water.

Psychiatrist

I let her climb her Escher hills.
She never learns. But she pays my bills.

The Victim

Camped by the lakeshore, she was dreaming
when it licked her ear—the rasp of tongue.
With its snout, it flipped her over, then, teeth out,
tore in. Pop of bubble wrap,
her knee opening. It held her down
to catch its breath, her shoulder in its mouth,
then surged forward, wanting her throat.
Thwarted by her arms, it sighed,
growled. Flayed the rest.

Someone found her, peeled.
The doctor joined what skin was left
to grafts from some dead cyclist,
dry as rice paper, with hieroglyphs inside.

She still has wavy hair and slender hips
and a slight limp, her level best.
She's twirled a heart or two, turned
to catch her name in someone else's mouth.
Don't speak to her of what she doesn't have,

her days aren't strange or sad. She loves her work
arranging tours for local art museums.
Sometimes she sickens at a thought, or some smell,
and won't be cornered. She did not choose
this life but here she is. Just like you.

Survivor

The stories don't matter. I know you
are confused, angry. You're being asked to care.
This is what poems do.

Below the water there are others,
in caverns worn smooth with crying.
She had a nice tongue, would lick my ear.
And then I woke up. As if the middle

of my life were a camping trip. I woke up,
light hitting something orange
on the far side of the lake. My old tent.

4

The Itza Bird

At dawn, with open wings
it landed

and strode precisely
with bobbing plume

and yellow eye
to see if I

was frog
or foe.

I was alone.
First light stumbled in

and I started to sing
louder, O louder!

And everyone came out
to hear it happen.

Birdwatcher's Fieldnotes

Dawn

Indigo turnstone
Ruddy bunting
Jub-Jub
Bufflehead
sree sree sree
A little bit of bread and no cheese

Midmorning

Willow ptarmigan
Barnacle goose
Salt peanuts
Quail's eggs in a monogrammed kerchief
Tunnock's Teacakes

Early Lunch at the Pond

Charlie Parker
Pair of mute swans
Leftover Peking Duck
Canned peaches with honey

Videophone

Petey Boy: sad
Sir Kiwi: standoffish
Patient you
twit twit

Nap in the Blind

Irony: the last dodo eaten by the last snow leopard
Bathos: the snow leopard choking on the bones
Khraaaa-khraaaa: Clark's nutcracker? Not here.
Dreamed Wittgenstein trying to screw a black swan

Afternoon

Dull clunk of the northern shoveler
Three lords and ladies
Cedar waxwing
The inevitable turkey vulture
Memory of zebra ducks and silvereyes in Queenie,
Willie wagtail's cartoon computer call,
Jacky winter on a rail—
I too was a post-sitter

Toward Marsh and River

A dancing killdeer
Surprising *peep* of dunlin
Solitary whimbrel
Croak overhead: Caspian terns

Note to Self

Practice muscovy duck routine:
Breathy male, trilly coo of the ladybird.
Deploy (iPhone)

Teatime at the Bishop's Finger

Wild Turkey
Potato skins, gin rummy
Caged bananaquits and paddyfield warblers—probably illegal
The barmaid: a crimson chat
Dik-it dik-it — check check
Complimentary Baby Duck
Offered, declined.
Jim Beam

Twilight Walk to the Hotel

Zeppelin puff of a courting cowbird,
half-out of human range.
Inaudible is not unheard.

In My Room

Skreek of traffic outside
Churchill's *Things in History That Interested Me*
Tweety and Sylvester (TV)
Phoebe in my window
Brandy tipple

Dinner at the Hoary Cockatiel

Big bird, fluffy mash, buttered veg
Creak of wine uncorking: gang-gang cockatoo?
A burrowing owl, sadly stuffed, on display

Videophone

"Come home soon"
You are my greater honeyguide

Insomnia Bucket List

Golden-olive woodpecker
Yellowhammers
Small cities of the sociable weaver
Jackie hangman's thorns
Shag in the Hebrides
Paradise flycatcher
Blackbird pie starting to sing
Barn swallow, soaring through the mead hall

Pelicans

Don't fool yourself: you don't know anything
about birds. So you've seen a documentary,
skimmed a book, can tell robins from chickadees.
You've stared across canyons, been pushed off a fence,
can guess what soaring is—falling in reverse—
but have you ever looked at a pelican?
Their beauty's folded awkwardness, red
lidless eyes, mouths baggy as inflatable pants.
Their webbed feet push the brakes mid-air,
like cartoon ducks'. No cormorants,
no sleek-arrow hunters, they wheel above the surf
and drop like a stack of twenty pancakes,
gulp at foam and fish, then struggle to
take off again. Drying out on shore, they
wonder what they've done to deserve
such graceful wings.

You should wish to be so brainless,
inefficient, beautiful. You drove past
them once, on your way to catch a plane.
Flying alone, no longer among them,
you've returned to knowing nothing
about birds, or who you are. Just eyeing
other people, wondering what you've done
to deserve this life. Your only one.

Lesson

My father returned after dark
when my sisters had given up hope
for a rough hug. Our mother read
by the streetlight that ran the stairs.

The door's click and slam froze me.
The sudden grip of homework undone,
trapped in the den with the TV on. He dragged
behind him a host of frigid air,

impatient for a gin and tonic, then more
tonic, then a slice of lemon.
Here ended the drive home.

Often he'd ask, wryly,
what I'd learned that day.

Tall, I guffawed once, seeing
myself in the fridge's long handle.
His ice cubes shattered
against the black window.

When my mother arrived
his look said, *Don't try me.*

Mistake

Everyone my parents liked was inside,
and outside the darkness held itself away
from the floodlights in the driveway,

and I stood there, looking for the one
sweet deathly girl who got me.
And, I swear on her name, *Derek*

I heard, and saw no one, she said
Derek, and I shivered a little, believing
I would believe and be carried away,

until *Derek, look up* came and I saw
my sister leaning from a small window
no one ever opened. *Why are you outside?*

Eclipse

One pin-holed sheet of aluminum,
one white card. We head to the park.

When the sky darkens, a crescent,
a fingernail, of light appears in our hands.

Around us, under a chestnut tree,
hundreds of tiny crescents.

All birdsong stops.
Old myths retake the day.

Libraries burn.
What we thought would last is gone.

1989

I painted houses by day—
phosphate bath and two heavy coats—

and at night her eyes put their English on me,
and the dark path of her hips in the circling neon,

the billiard clink of stubby bottles
palmed in the bush, down the ravine.

We sang so long a whole year went by.
Then our records started skipping,

repeating *I love you*
in basement rec rooms.

Red eyes, blue veins, a kiss
resisted between two trees.

I wanted a movie we could live in. From my ladder
I gazed across the geometric roofs,

the aquamarine swimming pools,
and wondered if I'd ever see her again.

That was us at seventeen.
Mist like a cat creeping up the lawn.

Winter Myth

A sloping house, a mother sick on the couch,
rumble of timber and china when trains go past.

Thwack of a Hespeler hockey stick on plywood.
Mute bump of rubber on a granite wall.

The lake ice so thick no auger could cut through,
the rocking jet-black water underneath, and smoke

from a chimney, the night outside warm
enough to stand in for hours but not enough

to get invited in. Cracks in the school.
And jeering boughs along the forest path,

banshee wind bullying snow across the road.
Such things turn into dreams of debt, a boy

idling by a river with a blank cheque
and a girl, the season's mind about to change.

Pomegranate girl, kissed to make her sad
and not loved. Though she was loved.

Angel Dust

I used to read Aesop when I was a boy.
In the dark home, awake,

I leaned out from the bed, cried out
at the bulging red eye underneath,

threw up at the sight. A shape
in shadow dragged another body

farther back, where a lone leg
moved faster, then fell asleep.

Staring into the growling dark
for years

I adjusted to this.
Accepted injustice.

Only light from long halls
makes sense of these things.

Eggs

The boy pushed his head up between two boughs and there it was,
round and brown on the next branch.

"Hey!" he whispered loudly, so as not to disturb the eggs. "I found a
bird's nest!"

"Okay, time out," said his eldest brother, jumping out of his own tree.

"Don't touch them," said his middle brother. "or they'll smell like you."

"But I don't stink," said the boy.

"You're a human being!" they hissed in reply.

There were two small light-blue eggs and one larger pale green with
brown spots.

It was noon. The lunch bell rang. They ran back inside for their
butter and baloney sandwiches.

"I hear you found a bird's nest," said the woman who made their
sandwiches.

"Yeah, and he almost touched the eggs!"

"I didn't!"

The boy told the woman about the different-coloured egg.

"Some birds lay their eggs in other birds' nests," she said.

"Why?" asked the boy.

"So they don't have to take care of them," she said.

"Why don't they want to take care of their own babies?"

"They're lazy!" she said, laughing.

"But they love their babies very much," said the boy.

She looked at him, a sad expression on her face.

A Country Tale

One night my great-grandfather got lost
in a storm, between the barn and the house.
The mountain snow snuffed the light.

He turned back to the barn, not
fifty yards behind him uphill and
slept the night between cows. In
the morning he crunched home

and made plans to sell the house,
the barn and all the rest. His wife
didn't say a word. It was war,
there was no help, they moved on.

Zombies

Love, stop collecting. Please change.
But you don't seem able to give up—

keep turning over chits of who we were:
a fur hat, ticket stub, dried flowers,
the Henry James you didn't read.

All is fear, lost joy, and never-sleep
—and I can't stop looking:
I'm a hawk in some old tapestry
eyeing the bodies below my tree.

Grey

Spread wings of a brained gull.
Drained and weather-beaten, dull.

A forest beetle struggles through the ash.
Open barrels of potash.

A charcoal suit lies in a hearse.
Gallery bomb of a poet's verse.

Wood-smoke's listless curlicue—
what's left of what you thought you knew.

5

Egyptian Archers

In Egyptian art, one archer stands
for all archers,

their contour drawn from his thigh, his shin, his chest,
his bow and quiver,

a deck of desires slightly spread.
Archers are technicians; this frieze

shows their discipline, how they draw
as one, their almond eye a blank,

calm as the strings unsmile,
sure of their mission

the moment their missiles
release.

They think: soon

I will recline with my lover and lyre again,
the bow's tension gone,

the twang become strum
and gentle stroking, the hand that leads

not hungry for battle's bloody plain, but
parting curtains, softly, to a bed

where my quiver will subside, incense slowly rise,
and the drum only of rain and conversation,

not war, nor plucked Assyrian eyes.
This arrow will save my life.

At the Dacha

Peter's grandmother complains
about the woodpile his father left there

years ago. Soft and mossy, it crumbles
the way an old lady can humble you

talking of Polish youth lost in the war.
She wants it to disappear

before it catches fire.
Clear a path, Piotr.

Catching, the chainsaw changes pitch.
There's something written
in the deep green fur,

something about human error.
Reset, the biting chain

erases whatever words.
Maybe it said, Start again.

If the Great Gatsby Had Children

Summer nights, he'd pace West Egg
making plans: granite boulders and hired hands
would stop the water eating his land.

Daisy would cross her arms. Success. All talk
vaguely a waste, he'd purse his lips.
Their boys—three tall, awkward ships—

would return each summer from boarding school
to race the seawall's white top,
shoot starlings, learn to sail yachts—

until they too succumb, over the years
to a Buchananian state of mind,
brilliant failures in a gin-soaked time

telling butlers to pack their bags, we're visiting Mommy,
applauding the well-dressed Thanksgiving turkey
then walking Daddy's wall, each on his own

wondering what their father had buried beneath,
what loving element was missing, or lost,
what justice staved off.

Florida

Sweaty Christmas, soggy, voluptuous end of land,
fat roots, fungus on the trunks, and alligator heads,
blue skies and the eye of water,
and water, and more water,

sand dollars and sun dollars, tattooed
men leaping like dolphins,
swamped galleons where downed planes should be—
and you in your checkered bikini, your shades open.
And your legs.

But nothing's the same anymore in this
world of waving palms.
The bird with a broken wing finds a thicket
deeper and darker than death to hide in.
And the water rises, brooding, German,
to take back old losses.

Moonlight

The moon like a mottled lambskin drum.

Tortoise-shell glasses tap shut
on a shiny brown table.

A slick tongue of headlamp.
My windows full of dying stars.

Two she-wolves, grounding a hind.

Dwindle, Dwindle

Dwindle, dwindle dying star
How alone you think you are

Carousel or spinning rock
Dwindle, dwindle icy luck

Dwindle, dwindle word and thought
Forget the things that you've been taught

No more high-gloss metaphor
Miming hands on Old Tom's floor

Ironic days with friends like these
No more straw Thucydides

Identifying the Body

Some guy leads me underground
to the place without shadows, where no one gets out—

all orange toes and humming lights,
lab coats, preservation-hall smells

and I know this is hell, cleaned up
for tourists like me.

Polite as an angel on a needle,
he asks if UI covers me for his form and if I am ready.

No dental records—who'd stoop to that for you.
No photos owned since the second fire.

No family—at least that's normal.
They tried to remove the bloated

jet look, he says, that's what the water does.
You're naked, in no-man's land. Alone.

It is you, with nothing
mussed, except maybe your soul.

This is what religion is for.
This moment.

Hate swells in me for all their "help"
—I cannot take you with me.

In their concrete bunker you're still a stigma,
lower than a syringe. And they

need to know: Were you alive
or dead when you fell in, or did someone push,

or maybe you did it to yourself. That's what they think.
You'll never get a proper burial now.

Orpheus

Was my task simply to coax you lightward
with sweet singing—or to learn
the secret name of suffering
as I strummed "My Way" through the sulphur?

For even though at the cave exit
light returned, the dark stayed
in our mouths. So when I turned to greet
the one I loved, the one I led

was no longer you: the face held
within the shroud, a white puppet—
small shoulders, bonier, a fixed grin.

Was this my punishment?
The wind chuckled, and I understood
my twee songs weren't enough:
you were—I had already—lost.

I must walk the length of my life
yammering about patience, joy and love
until I hated singing
and hated you.

Last Fare, Early Morning

Before the sun breaks they raise
an arm, say Take me

across the river. Stockbroker, stumbler,
nightshifter, young mother—

fall into backseat
sleep, then moth-like from the shadows

jerk up, with no more wings
to hide under,

only eyes in a mirror.

Reasons for Quitting

My name was Derek.
At thirty, a young lion ate me.

I exited onto a surface, a two-dimensional screen
of culture, math and strategy.

The faces smiled. I smiled back.
I was good at being reasonable.

Pears hung on the bows. Mouth said:
"That will make a good meal"

and if one fell I shouted: "Too late."
A lady arrived, a starling on a string

gripping the taut mauve of her shoulder,
blood trickle dry slate down her arm.

The bird shimmered and stared
and I went into its eye, underground,

asking if anyone knew my name.
Greenness filled me as she returned.

She asked, "Am I what you need?"
And I smiled and said yes

and accepted the grey drink.
Fade to bedpost and swell.

Light turned to dark, she said cut
and smoked in silhouette.

Her high-minded sister took over,
told me to cut it out and keep going.

At dawn, I found myself smiling, crying
in a glass patio door, considering

a reflection more substantial than I.
It pulled its left ear skeptically.

"Give me back my name," I said.
Pears oscillated in the tree.

"I will do better," I shattered.
It pulled its leaves skeptically.

The silence said "I don't care." I stumbled
into a child's picture book

of sandstorms and mimicry. I went blind.
You nuzzled my outstretched arm

and led me through sharp branches
back to my waiting, swollen body,

your voice a fox's ghostly call.
I think of him sometimes, still

lost down there, when I pass
shop windows on the street

and read the headlines
of this month's magazines.

Mockingbird

I don't need you to tell me why I'm here
or solve the mystery of how I slipped so far
and came to, lost in a snickering wood,
your trill my sole directive.

No bewigged guardian of the law
will ever compliment my patience, or sense
of beauty, or your eloquence.
Like you I'm playing with a kingless deck,
bound to songs that others made,
and with my life I sing out the pale result,
my reputation the heavy coat
of a Victorian postman.
Kindness makes me angry. It's rough justice.

Now we've reached the final, spoofing call
when you parrot the morning bell—
melody dug in, song-fuse set,
then that spine-deep tingle
that bursts in your abrupt last line,
enlightening darkness, slowing time.

ACKNOWLEDGEMENTS

I'd like to thank the many editors and staff who've put in the long hours required to publish literary journals and magazines in which my poems have appeared—including John Barton, Iain Higgins, Kim Jernigan, Pamela Mulloy, Barbara Carter, Daniel Nester, Ethan Paquin, Ross Leckie, George Sanderson, Peter Sanger, Don McKay, Robert Gibbs, Jan Zwicky, Michael Lista, Kevin Prufer, Moira MacDougall, Mary Jo Bang, Timothy Donnelly, Steven Schreiner and Eduardo Corral. Many of these poems have undergone changes in text and title since their original publication:

"After the Break-Up" in *The Collagist* 64; "Floating World" and "The Victim" (as "Survivor") in *The Malahat Review* 186; "Self-Timed Photograph" in *Canadian Literature* 129; "Necklace" (as "A Necklace in Space-Time") in *The New Quarterly* 133; "What Is A Watershed?" in *La Petite Zine* 8; "She-Wolf" (as "A Wolf") in *The New Quarterly* Spring 2000; "Widower" (as "Widower's Journal") in *Slope* 10; "Lesson" (as "Home") in *The Antigonish Review* 107; "Mistake" (as "Introduction") in *The Antigonish Review* 129; "A Country Tale" and "At the Dacha" in *The New Quarterly* 126; "Egyptian Archers" in *The Walrus* July/August 2013; "If the Great Gatsby Had Children" (as "The Sea-Wall") in *Pleiades Spring* 2000; "Mockingbird" in *Literary Review of Canada* November 2014. And "Flushing the Groundhog" in *Maisonneuve*. September 2015.

I'm also grateful to the fellow poets and writers who read my work once, twice or many times over the years, and whose considered responses have challenged and inspired me, including Mark Abley, Stephen Amidon, James Arthur, Erin Belieu, Bill Boswell, Anne Carson, Pablo Cantero, Jeremy Countryman, Lorin Cuoco at the International Writers Center, Theresa Daniels, Degan Davis, David Ferry, Wayne Fields, Jeremy Finkelman, William H. Gass, Maggie Helwig, Linda

91

Jenkins, Amanda Jernigan, Yusef Komunyakaa, Ross Martin, Charles
Newman, Heidi Lynn Nielsen-Nilsson, Jeff McRae, Christopher Miller,
Eric Ormsby, Eric Pankey, my MFA thesis advisor Carl Phillips, Doug
Sanders, Sean Singer, Amber Thomas, Mark Toft, Greg Vargo, Paul
Winner, and my wife, my life, Saleema (Nawaz) Webster.

Thanks also to Brian Trehearne, Maggie Kilgour, Gary Wihl, Stuart
Sherman and Steven Zwicker, great teachers of literature all, with whom
I had the privilege of studying at McGill University and Washington
University in St. Louis; and to the Montreal Writers Group—Maggie
Kathwaroon, Sarah Lolley, Paul Robichaud, Gina Roitiman, Elizabeth
Ulin—for keeping me writing through some difficult years.

A special thank you to James Pollock, whose jeweller's eye has helped
these poems shine as well as they can, and to my editor at Signal,
Carmine Starnino, who put me through the wringer, knowing I'd be
better for it.

Thank you, Pat and Norman, for everything. Thank you David,
Andrew, Gillian, Hilary, Vivienne, Saleema and Larkin.

Signal
EDITIONS

Carmine Starnino, Editor
Michael Harris, Founding Editor